W9-AZG-562

The First Lunar Landing

The
First Lunar
Landing

Dennis Brindell Fradin

Marshall Cavendish
Benchmark

New York

Marshall Cavendish Benchmark
99 White Plains Road
Tarrytown, NY 10591
www.marshallcavendish.us

Library of Congress Cataloging-in-Publication Data

Fradin, Dennis B.
The first lunar landing / by Dennis Brindell Fradin.
p. cm. — (Turning points in U.S. history)
Includes bibliographical references and index.
Summary: "Covers the first manned lunar landing as a watershed event in U.S. history, influencing social, economic,
and political policies that shaped the nation's future"—Provided by publisher.
ISBN 978-0-7614-4256-1
1. Project Apollo (U.S.)—Juvenile literature. 2. Apollo 11 (Spacecraft)—Juvenile literature. 3. Space flight to the moon—Juvenile literature.
4. Astronautics and state—United States—Juvenile literature. 5. Astronautics—Social aspects—United States—Juvenile literature.
I. Title. TL789.8.U6A533487 2010
629.45'4—dc22
2008034950
Photo Research by Connie Gardner
Cover photo by the Granger Collection
Cover: Astronaut Buzz Aldrin leaves the lunar module to begin his walk on the Moon.
Title page: A footprint left on the lunar surface by one of the Apollo 11 astronauts.

The photographs in this book are used by permission and through the courtesy of: *AP Photo:* NASA, 3, 32; 13, 31;
The Image Works: Jack K. Clark, 6; Mary Evans Picture Library, 16; NASA/SSPL, 39; *The Granger Collection:* 8; *Getty Images:* National Geographic, 14;
Corbis: 9, 28; Bettmann, 10, 12, 18, 20, 21, 24, 25, 26; NASA, Roger Ressmeyer, 27; Wally McNamee, 34; *Photo Researchers:* Science Source, 17, 22.

Timeline: AP Photo/NASA

Editor: Deborah Grahame
Publisher: Michelle Bisson
Art Director: Anahid Hamparian
Printed in Malaysia
1 3 5 6 4 2

Contents

The mysterious Moon dominated both the night sky and the imaginations of people from ancient times.

CHAPTER ONE

An Ancient Dream

Since ancient times, people have dreamed of visiting the Moon.

More than 1,800 years ago, the Syrian author Lucian wrote a tale about a **lunar** voyage. Lucian's hero travels in a boat that is lifted to the Moon by a waterspout. He discovers that the souls of dead people inhabit the Moon.

In his story *The Dream* (1634), German astronomer Johannes Kepler describes an odd lunar journey. Kepler's voyagers travel through space over a bridge that appears during an **eclipse**. On the Moon they meet creatures that look like a mixture of snakes and birds.

French author Jules Verne dreamed up another unusual way to visit the Moon. In Verne's novel *From the Earth to the Moon* (1865), a huge cannon

This colored engraving appeared in a nineteenth-century edition of Jules Verne's book *From the Earth to the Moon.*

shoots lunar travelers into space!

While writers explored space through stories and fantasy, astronomers were learning some basic facts about the Moon. The Moon is the heavenly body closest to Earth. It **orbits** our planet at a distance of about 240,000 miles (385,000 kilometers) away. The Moon is a lifeless world with no air or water.

In real life, a waterspout, bridge, or cannon could not transport people to the Moon. **Gravity** is in the way. This powerful force pulls objects toward heavenly bodies. For example, when you throw a ball up into the sky, Earth's gravity brings it back down. To overcome gravity, an object must move very fast. A spaceship bound for the Moon must travel at least 24,300

In the early twentieth century, French pilots experimented with this plane, which features seven layers of wings and a front-mounted engine and propeller.

miles (39,100 km) per hour to break loose from Earth's gravity.

The first airplanes were built in the early 1900s. They flew at less than 100 miles (160 km) per hour. To go to the Moon, we had to invent vehicles that could move at more than two hundred times that speed. Visiting the Moon was still only a dream.

Dr. Robert Goddard posed in a Massachusetts field in 1926 just prior to launching the fuel rocket he developed.

CHAPTER TWO

The Space Age Begins

In 1919 American scientist Robert Goddard published a paper. He predicted that powerful engines called rockets would take people to the Moon and beyond one day. People laughed at Goddard's suggestion. He was called "Moon mad."

Seven years later, in 1926, Goddard launched a rocket. It climbed just 41 feet (12.5 meters) high and traveled only 60 miles (96.5 km) per hour. Still, Goddard's 1926 launch marked the birth of modern rocketry.

In the following decades, scientists built more powerful rockets. The new machines rose many miles into the air. By the 1950s, rockets were reaching **altitudes** of 100 miles (160 km) and more—all the way to the edge of space.

Thirty years after Goddard's rocket launch, scientists developed huge guided missiles like this Redstone, built by the Army Ballistic Missile Agency.

The Space Age began on October 4, 1957. On that day the **Soviet Union** launched the first **artificial satellite**. *Sputnik 1*, a 184-pound (83.5-kilogram) aluminum sphere, orbited Earth at about 18,000 miles (29,000 km) per hour. The little satellite's altitude varied from about 140 miles (225 km) to nearly 600 miles (965 km) above our planet.

Americans were shocked that the Soviets had launched a satellite into orbit before they had. U.S. politicians and scientists decided to put more effort into space travel. *Explorer 1*, the first U.S. satellite in space, was

This scale model of the *Sputnik* satellite is displayed at the National Space Center in Leicester, England.

launched in January 1958. The Space Race—the era during which the United States and the Soviet Union competed at space exploration—had begun.

On May 25, 1961, President John F. Kennedy stated America's main goal in the Space Race. He said, "I believe this nation should commit itself to achieving the goal, before this decade is out, of landing a man on the Moon and returning him safely to the Earth." The 1960s would end in less than nine years. Achieving a manned lunar landing by late 1969 would be a great challenge.

An artist's drawing shows *Ranger 4*'s instruments being launched from its carrier high above the Moon's surface.

CHAPTER THREE

Step by Step toward the Moon

Meanwhile, both the United States and the Soviet Union had built rockets that could travel at least 24,300 miles (39,100 km) per hour. That was enough speed to make a lunar voyage. Both nations began to send unmanned devices called **space probes** to the Moon. The Soviet Union launched *Luna 2* on September 12, 1959. Two days later, *Luna 2* became the first probe to land on the Moon. The first U.S. probe to reach the Moon, *Ranger 4*, arrived on April 26, 1962. Over the next several years, the Americans and the Soviets sent more than twenty other probes that landed on or approached the lunar surface.

Besides sending out probes, the U.S. space agency, the National **Aeronautics**

The *Mercury 7* astronauts stand beside a 106-B plane, January 1961.

and Space Administration (**NASA**), also launched **astronauts** into space. These space explorers journeyed farther and farther from Earth. They brought their country steadily closer to its goal of landing people on the Moon.

In 1961 astronaut Alan B. Shepard Jr. became the first American in space. Shepard's spacecraft reached a height of 116 miles (187 km). Five years later, in 1966, astronauts Charles Conrad Jr. and Richard F. Gordon Jr. orbited Earth at a height of 850 miles (1,368 km). This was a record human flight altitude at the time.

American astronauts Frank Borman, James Lovell, and William A. Anders made a historic flight in 1968. Their *Apollo 8* craft took them all the way into lunar orbit. They became the first human beings to fly around the Moon. They then returned safely to Earth.

U.S. Navy swimmers hoist the *Apollo 8* module aboard the recovery ship, December 1968.

In May 1969, two Americans made the closest approach to the Moon anyone had achieved. *Apollo 10* astronauts Thomas Stafford and Eugene Cernan came within about 50,000 feet (15 km) of the lunar surface. Another 10 miles (16 km) and they would have landed on the Moon. The first attempt to actually do that would happen two months later.

The *Apollo 11* team, Edwin "Buzz" Aldrin, left, Neil Armstrong, center, and Michael Collins, stand outside a training capsule two months prior to their historic space mission.

Planning the First Manned Lunar Landing

By 1969, time was running out. Would President Kennedy's deadline be met? NASA decided to attempt a manned lunar landing that July with the *Apollo 11* mission. Three astronauts would serve as the crew. Neil A. Armstrong would be mission commander. Edwin E. "Buzz" Aldrin Jr. and Michael Collins would also go on the historic flight.

Since there is no air or water in space, *Apollo 11* had to carry these substances along. The astronauts also brought freeze-dried foods and space suits. The suits would protect the astronauts' bodies from extreme heat or cold and provide them with air when they walked on the Moon.

The plan was for *Apollo 11* to take the three-man crew into orbit around

Neil Armstrong

Neil Armstrong was born on August 5, 1930, near Wapakoneta in western Ohio. Armstrong fell in love with flying when he took his first airplane ride at age six. At fifteen he began taking flying lessons and paid for them by working in local stores. He was awarded his pilot's license on his sixteenth birthday—before he had a driver's license.

Armstrong became an expert flier. As a Korean War combat pilot and later as a test pilot, he was known for his coolness under pressure. He became an astronaut in 1962. Armstrong first flew in space in 1966 aboard *Gemini 8*. On that mission, he and David Scott completed the first manned docking of two space vehicles.

Armstrong's greatest moment came in 1969. When asked why the *Apollo 11* astronauts were attempting the dangerous voyage, Armstrong said, "I think we are going to the Moon because it's in the nature of the human being to face challenges. It's by the nature of his deep inner soul."

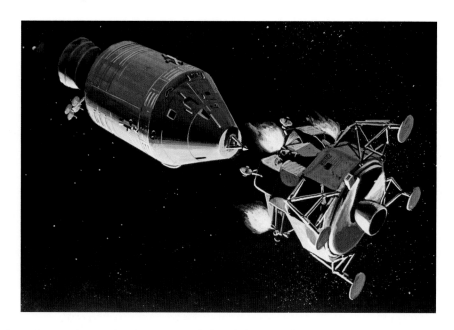

An artist's drawing shows how the lunar module, right, would separate from the command module during the *Apollo 11* mission.

the Moon. The spacecraft would then separate into two parts. The **command module**, *Columbia*, would orbit the Moon with Collins inside. The **lunar module**, *Eagle*, carrying Armstrong and Aldrin, would blast away from *Columbia*. *Eagle* would land Armstrong and Aldrin on the Moon. The two astronauts would explore the lunar surface. Then they would blast off from the Moon in *Eagle*. They would **dock** with *Columbia*, which would return the three men to their home planet.

The mission was very dangerous. If something went wrong, the astronauts might crash on the Moon, get lost in space, or burn up on their return to Earth.

During the prelaunch countdown, the astronauts leave Kennedy Space Center to ride a van to the *Apollo 11* spacecraft.

CHAPTER FIVE

The Trip to the Moon

More than a million people went to the Cape Canaveral, Florida, area to watch the launch of *Apollo 11*. Just past 9:30 A.M. on July 16, 1969, the NASA announcer began the final countdown:

Thirty seconds and counting. T-twenty-five seconds. Twenty seconds. Twelve, eleven, ten, nine, ignition sequence starts, six, five, four, three, two, one, zero. All engines running. Liftoff, we have a liftoff, thirty-two minutes past the hour. Liftoff on Apollo 11.

With a thunderous roar and brilliant flames, *Apollo 11* began its 250,000-

Countdown for the *Apollo 11* launch was conducted at the Launch Control Center, Firing Room 3, at Kennedy Space Center, Cape Canaveral, Florida.

mile (402,000-km) trip to the Moon. Within several minutes, the space-craft was more than 100 miles (160 km) high and was traveling at about 17,400 miles (28,000 km) per hour. Within several hours, the craft had reached a speed of about 24,300 miles (39,100 km) per hour—fast enough to tear loose from Earth's gravity.

"Hey, Houston," Armstrong reported to the NASA Mission Control Center in Houston, Texas. "This Saturn gave us a magnificent ride. It was beautiful!" Commander Armstrong was referring to the Saturn rocket that had carried *Apollo 11* into space.

"You are well on your way now!" responded Mission Control.

For three days, *Apollo 11* headed toward the Moon. Life aboard the

A beef and vegetable dinner, astronaut-style. The label also gives cooking instructions.

spacecraft was much different than it was on Earth. For one thing, there was no day or night. The Sun was always out, yet the sky was black. The astronauts could tell what time it was on Earth only by looking at their wristwatches and clocks. The astronauts were weightless in space. They slept in berths that prevented them from floating around the ship. They ate food from special plastic bags. When they had to go to the bathroom, they did so in special containers.

As they continued on, Earth looked smaller and smaller through the spacecraft's windows. The Moon loomed larger and larger. After fourteen hours, *Apollo 11* was nearly 100,000 miles (161,000 km) from home. As

Buzz Aldrin

Edwin Aldrin Jr. was born in Montclair, New Jersey, on January 20, 1930. His mother's maiden name was Marion Moon. Edwin had a little sister who had trouble saying the word *brother*. It came out sounding like "buzzer." People started calling him Buzz, which became his legal first name in 1988.

Aldrin served as a Korean War combat pilot. He also was highly educated, with a doctorate degree in astronautics. Methods that Aldrin devised for docking spacecraft were used on NASA spaceflights.

Aldrin became an astronaut in 1963. Three years later he flew in space aboard *Gemini 12*. In 1969 he became the second earthling to walk on the Moon. Aldrin later revealed that, while on the Moon, he had to go to the bathroom but couldn't wait to get back to *Eagle*. "Neil [Armstrong] might have been the first man to step on the Moon," Aldrin later said, "but I was the first to [relieve myself] on the Moon."

This close-up image of the lunar surface was taken from the command module *Columbia* while it orbited the Moon.

hours turned into days, *Apollo 11* reached distances of 175,000, 200,000, then 215,000 miles (281,500, 322,000, then 346,000 km) from Earth. After three days in space, *Apollo 11* entered a 60-mile-high (97-km-high) orbit around the Moon. Armstrong and Aldrin climbed into the *Eagle*, the lunar module that was supposed to land them on the Moon.

On the afternoon of July 20, the *Eagle* separated from the command module. Its two passengers, Armstrong and Aldrin, headed down to the lunar surface.

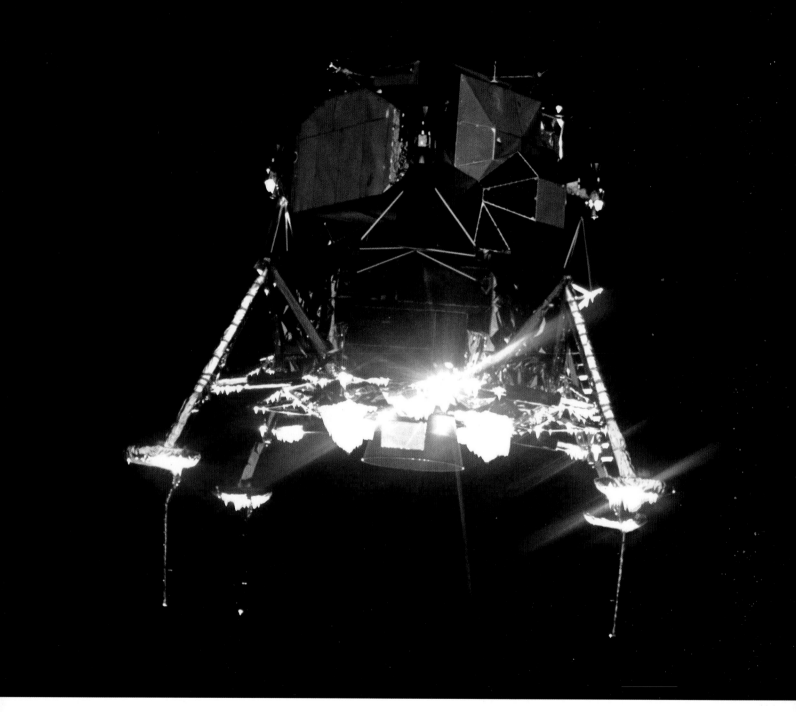

The *Apollo 11* lunar module *Eagle* descends to the Moon's surface.

CHAPTER SIX

"One Giant Leap for Mankind"

The descent to the Moon was the most dangerous part of the mission. If *Eagle* crashed or was damaged upon landing, Armstrong and Aldrin would be stranded on the Moon forever. Soon *Eagle* was so close to the Moon that Mission Control was reporting its height in feet:

Altitude 27,000 feet [about 5 miles, or 8 kilometers] . . . 21,000 feet . . . Altitude 13,500, Eagle, you're looking great. . . . Altitude 9,200 feet . . . Go for landing, 3,000 feet [900 m] . . .

As the module descended, Commander Armstrong spotted serious trouble.

The computer was landing *Eagle* in a dangerous spot—a cluster of large boulders. Armstrong took **manual** control of the *Eagle* and headed toward a safer landing place. *Eagle* was 200, 160, 40, then 30 feet (61 m to 9 m) above the lunar surface. At 4:17 P.M. Florida time on July 20, 1969, *Eagle* touched down on solid ground.

"Houston," a relieved Commander Armstrong reported, "The *Eagle* has landed!" Armstrong and Aldrin had become the first earthlings to land on another heavenly body.

Armstrong and Aldrin inspected *Eagle* to make sure it hadn't been damaged upon landing. They ate the first meal on the Moon. Then they put on their space suits. At 10:56 P.M. on July 20, 1969, Armstrong climbed down the stairs of *Eagle* and stepped onto the lunar surface.

"That's one small step for a man, one giant leap for mankind!"

"The Moon Show"

No TV crews or newspaper photographers went to the Moon with Armstrong and Aldrin. So how did Americans get to see TV images and photographs of the astronauts? Among the cargo that *Eagle* carried to the Moon were several cameras, including a TV camera that worked automatically.

Nearly a billion people worldwide watched the first Moon walk—a quarter of the world's population. Michael Collins was not one of those watching. With no TV onboard *Columbia*, Collins could not see the historic Moon walk.

Astronaut Buzz Aldrin walks on the Moon, July 20, 1969.

Armstrong said to the people watching on TV back on Earth.

Eighteen minutes later, Buzz Aldrin joined Armstrong on the lunar surface. Looking around the Moon, Aldrin said, "Beautiful, beautiful, beautiful! A magnificent **desolation**."

For about two hours, Armstrong and Aldrin moved about the Moon's surface. On Earth, each man would have weighed about 360 pounds (163 kg) in his space suit. The Moon, however, has just one-sixth the gravity of Earth. This means that each astronaut, including his space suit, weighed only 60 pounds (27 kg) on the Moon. As a result, Armstrong and Aldrin felt very light. They could make leaps and jumps that would be impossible on Earth.

Walking, running, and making what they called kangaroo hops, the two astronauts performed some important tasks. They collected lunar soil and rock samples to

Aldrin poses beside the American flag, brought on the mission to commemorate the historic lunar landing.

take back to Earth. They took photographs and set up scientific instruments. They placed an American flag on the Moon and unveiled a plaque. Commander Armstrong read the words on the plaque for viewers a quarter of a million miles (402,000 km) away:

HERE MEN FROM THE PLANET EARTH
FIRST SET FOOT UPON THE MOON
JULY 1969, A.D.
WE CAME IN PEACE FOR ALL MANKIND

Michael Collins

Michael Collins was born on October 31—Halloween—in Rome, Italy, in 1930. His father, an American army general, moved the family around a great deal. Growing up, Collins lived in Italy, Oklahoma, New York, Puerto Rico, Virginia, and Washington, D.C.

Collins became a U.S. Air Force pilot and then an astronaut. In 1966, on the *Gemini 10* mission, he became the third American to walk in space. In 1968 doctors discovered that he had a problem with his spine, and it required surgery. A year later, after a quick recovery, Collins served as command module pilot for the first Moon walk. He had to keep *Columbia* in proper lunar orbit during Armstrong and Aldrin's stay on the Moon. In addition, he had to perform the docking procedure with *Eagle* for the trip back to Earth.

Collins made an intriguing comment about the view from space. He said that seeing his home planet from so far away made him feel like an **"extraterrestrial** being."

After finishing their work, Armstrong and Aldrin returned to *Eagle*. They rested for a few hours. Then *Eagle* lifted off from the Moon. It successfully docked with *Columbia*, where Michael Collins awaited them. The return to Earth took three days. On July 24 *Columbia* splashed down in the Pacific Ocean near U.S. Navy ships that awaited the vessel. The rescue of the three astronauts from the ocean ended the historic mission that had landed the first men on the Moon.

The *Apollo 11* astronauts (from left to right) Armstrong, Collins, and Aldrin speak to the media from behind glass while aboard the USS *Hornet*.

CHAPTER SEVEN

A Turning Point

The safe return of the *Apollo 11* astronauts fulfilled President Kennedy's goal. The United States had landed men on the Moon and had brought them back home safely. The mission was completed before Kennedy's deadline—the end of the 1960s.

The *Apollo 11* mission was a turning point in U.S. history in several ways. At the time, Americans were bitterly divided over the Vietnam War. Many Americans favored U.S. involvement in the conflict. Many others, however, were opposed. Arguments over the war tore families apart and ended friendships. The Moon landing was an achievement that made almost all Americans proud. It provided a big boost to the spirit of the nation.

Moon Germs?

Scientists had a slight suspicion that the *Apollo 11* astronauts might have brought back germs from the Moon. Therefore, after returning to Earth, the three men were placed in **quarantine**. They lived away from other people in special laboratories for more than two weeks. Scientists finally concluded that the astronauts had brought back no Moon germs. They were released from a seventeen-day quarantine on August 10, 1969. Only then could they join the celebrations of their great achievement.

The Moon landing also proved that Americans could achieve almost anything by working together. About 400,000 people and 20,000 companies had made the lunar landing happen. Contributors ranged from cooks who prepared the astronauts' meals to scientists who designed the space suits.

In the early 1960s computers were huge. In fact, they filled entire rooms. Astronauts needed smaller computers for use on the Apollo missions. The smaller computers designed for the missions eventually went into general use. This means we have *Apollo 11* partly to thank for our modern computers that fit on a desk or in a pocket.

Apollo 11 ended the Space Race—at least as far as the Moon was concerned. The United States would forever have the honor of making the first manned lunar landing. The mission also helped launch a new era in space exploration. Michael Collins said that, from space,

Earth was "one unit" with no visible borders separating countries. A few years after the *Apollo 11* mission, the United States and the Soviet Union began cooperating on space missions. It started in July 1975, when an American spacecraft and a Soviet vessel docked together in space. Soviet **cosmonauts** and American astronauts exchanged flags, shared meals, and did experiments together. Since then, the United States has cooperated with a number of nations on space missions,

An American Achievement

The Soviet Union never fulfilled its plans to land people on the Moon. Even by 2009, the United States remained the only country to have achieved a human lunar landing.

MOON WALK MISSIONS

Because it was the first, *Apollo 11* remains the most famous manned lunar landing. Over the next few years, however, the United States landed men on the Moon five more times. The six Moon walk missions were as follows:

Apollo 11 July 16–24, 1969

Apollo 12 November 14–24, 1969

Apollo 14 January 31–February 9, 1971

Apollo 15 July 26–August 7, 1971

Apollo 16 April 16–27, 1972

Apollo 17 December 7–19, 1972

A Walk on Mars?

Many people expected that, within a few years of the Moon walks, the United States would begin sending astronauts to planets besides Earth. That did not happen, partly because interest in the space program waned. In fact, by 2011— thirty-nine years after the last manned lunar landing—human beings still had not visited any heavenly body besides the Moon. Sometime in the twenty-first century, however, a human mission will probably be sent to Mars. That should be very exciting. The Red Planet once had water on its surface. Long ago it may have been home to some forms of life. Mars may still harbor simple life forms today.

such as the International Space Station, a joint project involving more than fifteen countries.

Like other astronauts, the *Apollo 11* crew reported that the loveliest object in space was their home planet, Earth. "It seems like a very small, fragile, **serene** little sphere," said Michael Collins. A later lunar explorer, *Apollo 15* astronaut James B. Irwin, said, "The Earth is the only natural home for man that we know of, and we had better protect it."

Millions of people who have seen pictures of Earth taken from space feel the same way. As a result, the lunar landing program helped inspire the environmental movement that began around 1970. Fulfilling the ancient dream of exploring the Moon may ultimately help us heal the fragile environment of Earth.

On a *Challenger* mission in 1984, astronaut Bruce McCandless went free-flying in space above Earth's surface.

Glossary

altitudes—Heights; distances between sea level and a higher object.

artificial satellite—A man-made object that revolves around a heavenly body.

astronautics—A science involving the construction and operation of spacecraft.

astronauts—Space travelers.

command module—A portion of a spacecraft in which astronauts live and communicate with Earth.

cosmonauts—Soviet or Russian space travelers.

desolation—Barrenness; lifelessness.

dock—To join two spacecraft in outer space.

eclipse—An event that occurs when one heavenly body moves in front of another.

extraterrestrial—From a world beyond Earth.

gravity—The force that pulls objects toward heavenly bodies.

lunar—Relating to the Moon.

lunar module—The portion of a spacecraft that lands on the Moon.

manual—Operated by hand.

NASA—The U.S. space agency (National Aeronautics and Space Administration).

orbits—Moves in a circular or egg-shaped path around another object.

quarantine—A state of isolation in which people or animals are kept apart from others to prevent the spread of disease.

serene—Quiet and peaceful.

Soviet Union—A country that was made up of Russia and several surrounding states. It was disbanded in 1991.

space probes—Unmanned devices that send data from outer space to Earth.

Timeline

1903—Americans Orville and Wilbur Wright make the first successful airplane flights.

1919—American scientist Robert Goddard publishes a paper predicting that rockets will one day take people to the Moon.

1926—The launch of a small rocket by Robert Goddard marks the start of modern rocketry.

1957—The Soviet Union launches the first artificial satellite, *Sputnik 1*, beginning the Space Age.

1958—The United States launches *Explorer 1*, its first artificial satellite.

1959—The Soviet Union's *Luna 2* becomes the first space probe to land on the Moon.

1961—**April:** Soviet cosmonaut Yuri Gagarin becomes the first human being to orbit Earth.
May: Astronaut Alan B. Shepard Jr. becomes the first American in space; President John F. Kennedy challenges the United States to land a man on the Moon by 1969.

1903   *1926*   *1958*   *1961*

1962—*Ranger 4* becomes the first U.S. space probe to land on the Moon.

1966—Astronauts Charles Conrad Jr. and Richard F. Gordon Jr. orbit Earth at a height of 850 miles (1,368 km)—a record altitude at the time.

1968—*Apollo 8* astronauts make the first manned spaceflight to orbit the Moon.

1969—On July 20, *Apollo 11* astronauts Neil Armstrong and Buzz Aldrin make the first manned lunar landing while Michael Collins orbits the Moon.

1972—In December, *Apollo 17* astronauts land on the Moon. This is the sixth and final manned lunar landing of the twentieth century.

2009—The world celebrates the fortieth anniversary of the *Apollo 11* lunar landing.

1969

2009

Further Information

BOOKS

Crewe, Sabrina, and Dale Anderson. *The First Moon Landing*. Milwaukee: Gareth Stevens, 2004.

Kuhn, Betsy. *The Race for Space: The United States and the Soviet Union Compete for the New Frontier*. Minneapolis: Twenty-First Century Books, 2007.

Thimmesh, Catherine. *Team Moon: How 400,000 People Landed* Apollo 11 *on the Moon*. Boston: Houghton Mifflin, 2006.

Woodford, Chris. *Moon Missions*. Milwaukee: Gareth Stevens, 2005.

W E B   S I T E S

For exciting material about the race to the Moon with links pertaining to the *Apollo 11* crew, liftoff, lunar landing, and first Moon walk, along with a Buzz Aldrin interview:
http://teacher.scholastic.com/space/apollo11/index.htm

For a variety of data and pictures concerning the *Apollo 11* mission from NASA:
http://history.nasa.gov/ap11ann/introduction.htm

For a great deal of information about lunar exploration, including the *Apollo 11* mission:
http://nssdc.gsfc.nasa.gov/planetary/lunar

Bibliography

Barbour, John. *Footprints on the Moon*. New York: Associated Press, 1969.

CBS News. *10:56:20 PM EDT, 7/20/69: The Historic Conquest of the Moon as Reported to the American People by CBS News Over the CBS Television Network*. New York: Columbia Broadcasting System, 1970.

Chaikin, Andrew. *A Man on the Moon: The Voyages of the Apollo Astronauts*. New York: Viking, 1994.

Hurt, Harry III. *For All Mankind*. New York: Atlantic Monthly Press, 1988.

Koppeschaar, Carl. *Moon Handbook: A 21st-Century Travel Guide*. Chico, CA: Moon Publications, 1995.

Shepard, Alan, and Deke Slayton. *Moon Shot: The Inside Story of America's Race to the Moon*. Atlanta: Turner Publishing, 1994.

Wagener, Leon. *One Giant Leap: Neil Armstrong's Stellar American Journey*. New York: Forge, 2004.

Index

Page numbers in **boldface** are illustrations.

About the Author

Dennis Fradin is the author of 150 books, some of them written with his wife, Judith Bloom Fradin. Their book for Clarion, *The Power of One: Daisy Bates and the Little Rock Nine*, was named a Golden Kite Honor Book. Another of Dennis's well-known books is *Let It Begin Here! Lexington & Concord: First Battles of the American Revolution*, published by Walker. Other recent books by the Fradins include *Jane Addams: Champion of Democracy* for Clarion and *5,000 Miles to Freedom: Ellen and William Craft's Flight from Slavery* for National Geographic Children's Books. Their current project for National Geographic is the *Witness to Disaster* series about natural disasters. *Turning Points in U.S. History* is Dennis's first series for Marshall Cavendish Benchmark. The Fradins have three grown children and five grandchildren.